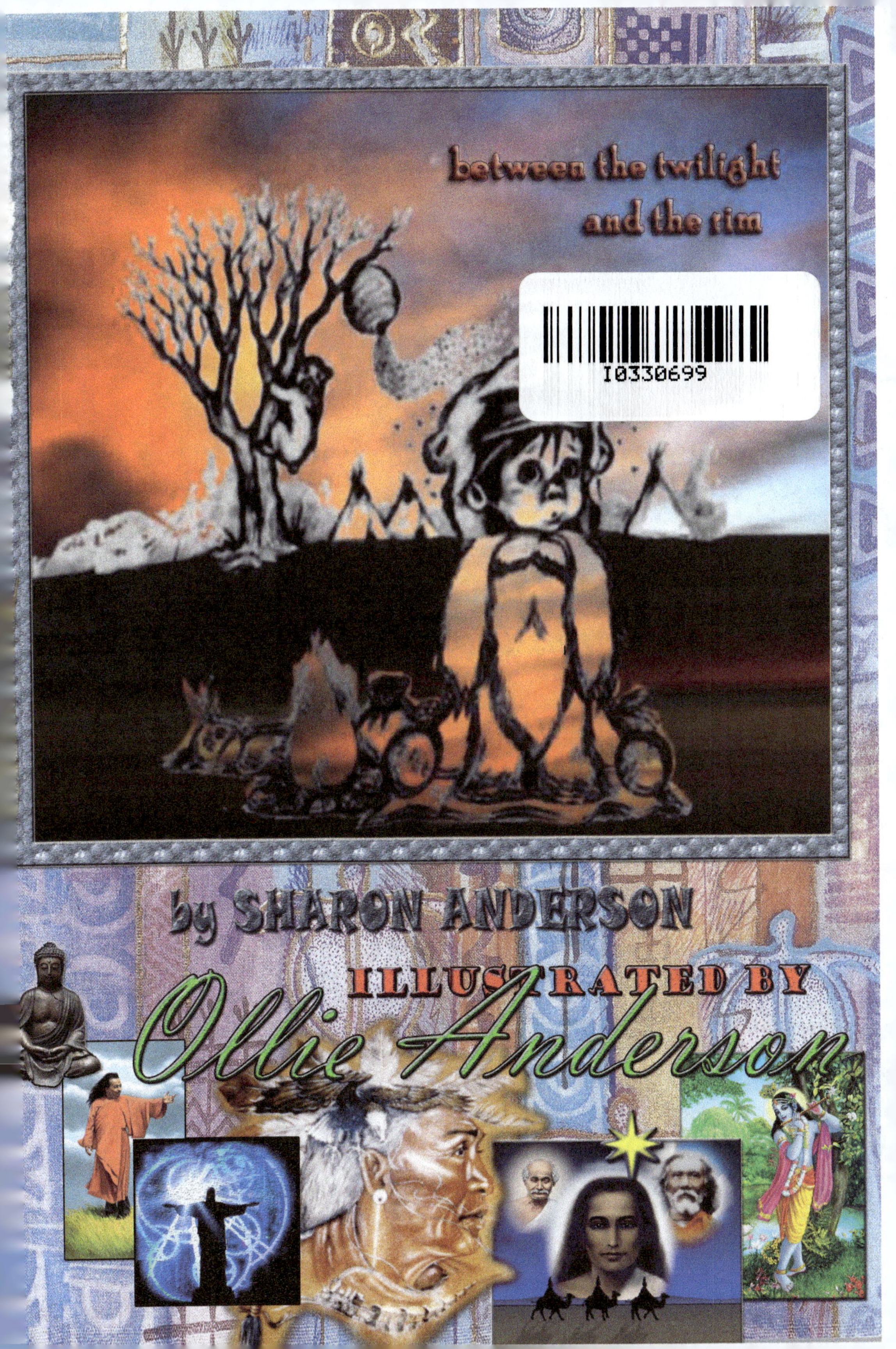
between the twilight
and the rim
I0330699
by SHARON ANDERSON
ILLUSTRATED BY
Ollie Anderson

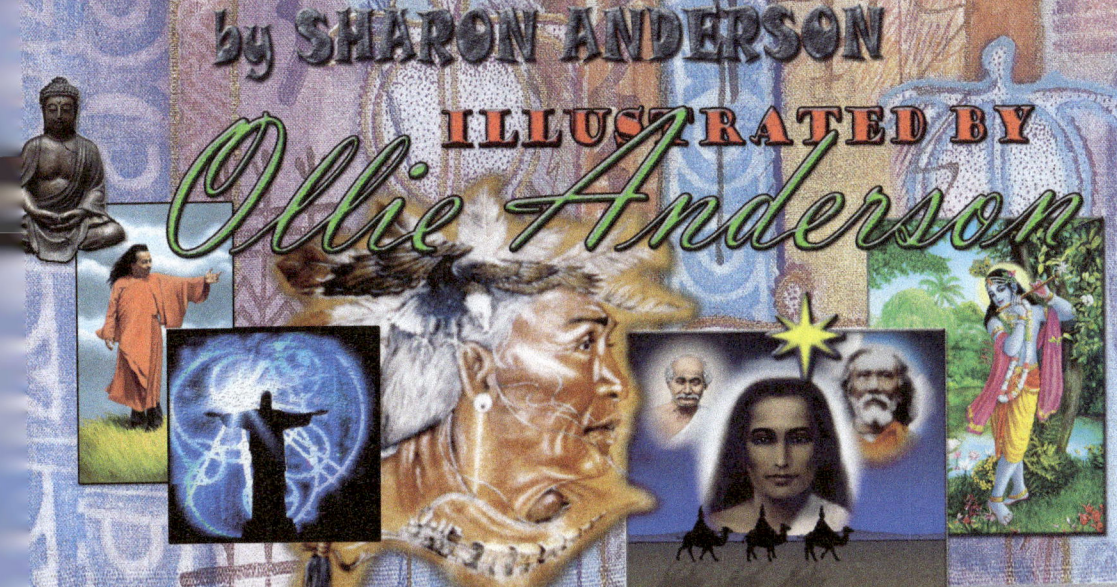

by Sharon Anderson

and illustrated

by Ollie Anderson

Dear Sharon:

Your beautiful and sweet letter gave me a chuckle this morning. You are so dear. I'm glad you enjoyed my novel and that it inspired you to finish writing yours. I only read a few pages of it because Miriam only printed a few to show me. However, I look forward to reading the rest of it. Ollie's pictures are perfect. You make a good team: writer and illustrator. love,
swami

NK/nm   Wed, Mar 20, 2013 09:30 AM

Inspired by the teachings of
J. Donald Walters;
Swami Kriyananda
And Guru
Paramahansa Yogananda

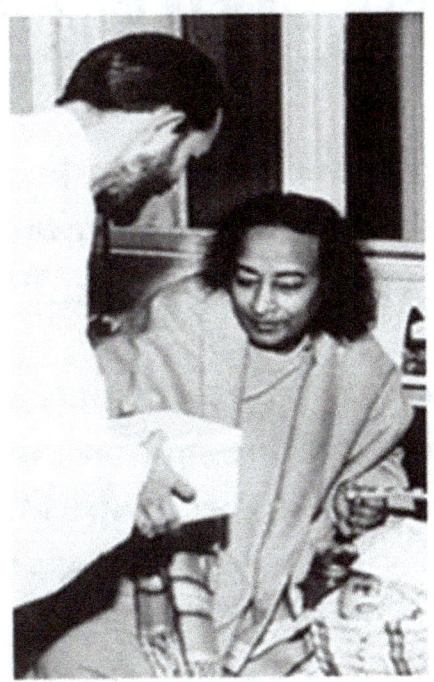

The meditative life and the search for God
are encapsulated here in a story.
It is not the saga of a renowned saint or sage,
but the simple and pure expression of love
in a small native boy
as he discovers truths that blossom
out of his own ancient traditions,
and are experienced anew.

Ali sets out from the prairies of his homeland
through a settlement of town-folk,
and far beyond,
seeking to become a man.
He learns that in the process,
finding happiness is the key.

This story is illustrated with a beautiful vibrancy,
full of wonderfully charming characters and color,
by Sharon's sister Ollie.

They grew up in northwestern Canada
where the pristine majesty of nature
would serve as the perfect inspirational backdrop
for this timeless wilderness quest.

A story is a good way
to display deep truths
Not only children love stories

BETWEEN THE TWILIGHT
AND THE RIM
ISBN 9780692338612
9780692338056 E-Book

BETWEEN THE TWILIGHT AND THE RIM

Contents

Introduction

    A spiritual adventure/A yogic teaching

Part I

    I am One

Part II

    Finding Happiness

Part III

    Guru

Suggested further reading and resources

PART I

Grandfather, do all holy people experience the same God?

Of course.. Truth is truth

..What is the truth?

that God brought everything into existance out of Himself

So, is there only one God?

Yes, The one in you And everywhere

"I AM ONE". The words shimmered and spread out as if to cross the sky with the wind. Aliheli woke slightly, and shifted his head out of the sunlight a bit, then remembering that he was on a trail in the big basin, slid back into his sleep. Far over to the right between two grass-sloped mountains, was a big ceremony.

Many hundreds of warriors were dressed in their finest and in perfect rhythm together were pouring their hearts skyward in song, as they lumbered softly in a circular pattern with their feet, drifting to the left and right as if to catch a wisp of wind into flight. How beautiful was the sun sinking behind burly clouds lined with red tinges on grey. What was left of the blue in the sky had become luminous and bright at the top of a fiery hearth beaming out of the twilight shadows.

What was moving amidst it all? Aliheli focused on a swirling mass suspended in the air above the celebration. It was Grandfather moving towards the opening of sky --in a magnificent offering. His noble brow and chiseled face stretched toward the heavens, and began dissipating..becoming the very landscape itself.

Then the breezes began to gather into a sweeping motion pressing down on the prairie grasses until all fell into a gentle force of quiet at the forefront. The pulsing of voices and motion became trails of background tinkling, and a hum of pure contentment pervaded the valley. I AM ONE. The words arose again, absorbing the dream and everything in it. They began to swell toward the sunset on all sides. Aliheli woke to a warm thrill all along his spine, and a smile on his lips.

"What does it mean, I wonder.." He couldn't ask Grandfather, for Aliheli was some 18 miles away from the village, on a quest to become a man. Although only 11 years in age, he was a boy of intense yearning and curiosity. He had been raised steeped in the wonderment of the ancient traditions of his tribe, and the boy had firmly resolved to faithfully follow a thread of truth he had perceived in his nature from an early time. It was a deep longing to find out who he indeed, really is. The elders in the village finally gave in to the boy's persistent requests to fulfill an ancient practice of sending a young one into the wilderness to find his own way when he is ready. Grandfather gave the final blessings.

Ali couldn't really explain what this truth was or where it would lead him. He only knew to give it his unswerving and ultimate dedication. He knew it made him want to seek quiet. When he could become still enough, there it would be. He would find cozy clearings in the forest where he could nest in a bed of pine needles and peer out of a glade of evergreens into a great light that would softly surround him. And then with his eyes closed, that light would transform and begin to express itself – growing into a calm happy feeling, and feeding him noble thoughts. He felt in those very thoughts, the thrill of being firmly rooted.. but not only as he the boy.. When he was settled in this way, he was nature itself, satisfied with the day that was existing within him, and pleased to be the offering of life that was gathered there. Aliheli knew he, as a boy --was part of the scene.. but this feeling that it was so much bigger than just he ..well, that's what made it so thrilling. Just feeling you are a creation that grows, and ebbs and flows within the tides of all that lives.. it was enough to make him happy. It made his a life with no boundaries. .. Deep within he felt as a flower opening up to the sun. Then he could be the sun too..for, somehow, everything around him seemed to vibrantly invite his reaching heart to enter,embrace, and become it. Sometimes at home he had wandered away from the other children to seek this feeling also in the tall grasses. They were such a friendly place to dream. And just as waking from a dream in the mornings to the greater awareness of being a boy living in a village, these feelings allowed in him a further awakening even from that -- the boy living in a village came to understand he too was in a dream, on another level, and he could wake up even further, to the awareness of an even grander place.. one that **he** could be the creator of, once he figured out how..

Well, enough of going deep inside his thoughts. It was indeed morning, and a new adventure with it, awaited him. He rolled up his bear pelt blanket, and walked to the stream to get a fresh drink of water. There were some Saskatoon berries growing near the river, and they made a delicious breakfast. Aliheli well knew how to set a rabbit snare, but he didn't have the heart to hurt a little rabbit. It was like snatching a piece out of his dream body to do so. The little rabbits quivered so, and lived in fear of all those larger animals who would lurk and wait for the chance to pounce. That's the thing, Aliheli knew what it was like to be the rabbit. The folk-lore of his ancestors told of this knowledge from times before teachings were even written down, but no one seemed to follow the path of these teachings to their truest meanings anymore. But deep inside, yes, Aliheli knew what it was to be the rabbit. Their moments in the sun were lovely, but short lived. Much of their lives were spent shivering in the shadows. Aliheli followed the river along happily and finally around noon, set down his traverse sticks, and sat to recount all he had seen and felt along the winding river. There was a bee hive up high in a tree behind him. Honey would make a nice lunch. He looked up to the point between his eyes. That is where he was able to find answers. He thought of the bear, who was the master at getting honey.

He had once been a bear.. this he was sure of. But, that was long before he had discovered that answers could appear in his own head.. at this spot that seemed to bring all of nature together for him, and give him answers intuitively.

When he thought only at his heart, or in his lower 'reasoning' mind at the back of his head, everything and everybody in the world seemed separate, and divided – finding answers were like puzzles that had to be put together. But here at the point between the eyebrows was something that had evolved for him when finally he had reached the level of being a human person. It was a free opening into thoughts of a higher order. Here, he was aware of being separate only for the purpose of understanding that something was wrong..he had drifted away from being the whole of the great Spirit, and had somehow settled for being just a little misplaced part of it. Long ago as the bear too, he had known that something was wrong. He was hungry.. but he wasn't aware that he was a thing which felt the hunger. He only knew the hunger itself existed, and acted instinctively. The person finds himself quite aware of the pain of being a separate thing. Aliheli has been aware of this greatest of hungers, and it has served to get him onto the trail of finding out how he can become one with the great Spirit again, where all nourishment for his soul is supplied. When he would become confused in his search, he would ever more tightly cling to this thread of truth that he somehow belonged to the Great Spirit.. and it led him again and again to the point between the eyebrows; the frontal lobe that the bear and rabbit didn' t have. Aliheli was happy to have found it because there was no puzzle there. He can still be somewhat like the bear; hibernating in a contentment where there are no questions.. just answers. But, because he was now a person and not an animal, this hibernation was on a different level completely. He wasn't having a peaceful sleep, he was finding peace while being more awake than he'd ever been. No longer did he- the bear, have to trudge instinctively toward a higher existence in an automatic but painfully slow evolution. He had gotten stung on the nose so many times, and felt hunger so often. It took much time, and the natural course of things but he did evolve into a being that could begin realizing he was a **"thing"** that could experience hunger. He wasn't just the hunger itself. He could do things for himself. This gradual knowledge of "self" served to bring him into the bodies of ever-deeper thinking human beings, and finally he found himself in the body of Aliheli many lives later. Now that this awareness of being separate had served its purpose, he was ready to finally start the last leg in the journey ; getting home. Ali opted for some dried pemmican out of his pack and some rhubarb stalks he found nearby for supper finally, and left the bees to their honey. He travelled a little farther that day, and enjoyed the many colored wild flowers on their sunny slopes. Then he laid down and opened his heart. "Oh, Master", he whispered softly.." don't ever be even a breath away from me..". He settled in for the night, feeling the thrill of being watched over by One who gently stroked his face with the moonbeams in an ever deepening love.

Ali woke to the sound of a faraway bell. It was a beautiful morning..there were twinkling rays of light squeezing in through his eyelids. The bell was deep..it was more a memory than a sound.. a memory that vibrated a warm feeling into his blood stream from his heart. He lay on his back and opened his eyes. The Great Spirit was still upon him, close and warm. Ali giggled a little.. the Spirit was in a playful mood. How are you going to show yourself today, beautiful Sir? Ali asked out loud. He calmed his heart and went there with his attention. He saught out the bell sound once again and settled there. It took some time tuning in, and a kind of intense sinking into silence, but the the bell's gong started to chime in and began to stretch out a little stronger with each ring. It started to warble in and out with a whoooshhh eeeyeeeahhhh.. as if it was drifting far to one side and then tumbling back on a roll. This was fun. Ali sat up and looked off toward the canyon. He closed his eyes and felt his eyelashes tickling with a cool wisp of air. Do you love me? He asked softly. "Whoooooahhhh..eeeyyeeeeahhh ..oahhhh.. Oh, yeeeeesss.. The forest was so beautiful.. the air felt like a breath of heaven brushing by him.. Ali felt as he had when he was a little papoose. How does one know what you love, and what loves you?..everything **was** that love.

How could you differentiate it, or separate it into just one thing. He stood up and with his arms out, twirled in a circle, laying his head back and relaxing into the pretty morning. Will you take care of me? He asked..

There was no answer, but when he turned around there was a trail he hadn't noticed, into a thick, mossy forested area. It bent down a hill and around. He fancied himself a Brave hunting, and scooted down the trail in a trot. It felt good to run, so he kept going. He found the mouth of a cave, and venturing inside, he could feel a cool clamminess. But it was an intriguingly ominous mood that was being created, and so he let it lure him on farther inside. The thought occurred to him suddenly that the wolf may be in here; ..the **other** hunter. Oh, he thought..I didn't really **want** to hunt. I **like** deer, just to look at. He didn't want to compete with any wolf. But it was too late. A marked swing in his attitude began to nag at him, that there was a little more danger here than adventure. What if the wolf turned on him..some hunter he would be then.. He felt more and more like a little boy fearing the shadows of the bare trees as they swished against the walls of his room and made a scratchy sound . He used to image that they were growing knarley bones and trying to break through the window. All at once Ali remembered why he was here. With all his heart, he put the thought in his head that it is God he wants, not a thing more. He is not here to hurt a fly, and will not dwell a minute longer in this hunter mood.. He came here following his Beloved ..who was **supposed** to be answering his question, by the way.. about if he **cares** for me. Well, do you? He asked loudly and sharply, as if to clear a spot for relief to descend. Sure enough, the rustling of leaves became as a trill of laughter behind him, and turning around, saw the sun had shifted to mid morning, landing close enough to the opening of the cave, that a sliver of pretty white light was drawing a thin bolt along the rock inside. It made a candl-ey kind of light, very cozy and inviting. Now the cave seemed like the perfect place to make a little rock worshipping alter, and he took some sage out of his pocket to burn there. He thought of the love that was humming in his heart as being an aromic kindling, drawing his dear One nearer.. He stayed there for a long time, and happiness seemed to seep into his skin from without and melt into his insides. He would love to be here forever he thought. Then suddenly with a little puff of air, the final corner of his sage fire was blown out and he looked contently at one little ember. He imagined the ember as a seed, and then his seed too, became caught up in a light puff of air, and swirled its way out of the cave..ever higher and higher into the fresh air.. what fertile soil many miles away .. what absolutely wonderous place would it be carried off to? he wondered..Well, the sky is the limit, he said with a sigh.   And then delightedly he squealed Hah!!. I know who you are today.. all along I should have seen it..you are the wind! That was a wonderful game. And I know now that you do care for me and always take care of me, if I let you. I didn't have to feel any danger in the cave for long. All I had to do was turn to you, and look what happened instead. Oh, I do love you so!

Ali began walking the trail again. Now, about the bell..he thought. It had been luring him from within. Somewhere in the lives he has lived..there **has** been a lovely bell ringing. He thought about moors and castles, morning mists in the glen.. in a time long past. How tranquil were these thoughts. Wait, he remembered a bell he got to hear as a little boy once, in a settlement not far the other side of the Enoch reservation. It was a little town called Dunkirk. He certainly didn't have to be home for supper..Come, Great Spirit, he said..lets go find us a real bell!

Ali felt so free as he ambled down a pretty willow strewn road.. he stretched his neck back and took in the air. It was like a nectar. Stopping there, he let the sun shine full on his face.. and remembered Grandfather quoting him the great words of the Master Jesus who said that **man does not live by bread alone but every breath that comes from the mouth of God.** The tiny little sunlight electrons mixed with the bursting molecules of fresh air, trickled through him-- filling his trunk through to his limbs with vigor. But more than that .. happiness. Ahh, how wonderful --he was going somewhere. And, he thought to ask at that very moment. Great Spirit of my Grandfather, will you come? I seek to find you in different places and in different cultures. I want to see how you attend to my brothers and sisters of different origins, and different upbringings. And Sir, he paused.. I long to show you to all I meet.. oh I will try not to boast. But you are like a trophy.. as the treasure unearthed in the field. And I would sell my horse and saddle and leave my home.. just to be with you..always. He smiled. Presently the sky began to dreamily soften and darken with a velvety purple tinge around the edges. Finally a faraway hill presented an array of shooting light beams through a mist emanating from something hidden behind. "Come see", it was beckoning with brilliant swooning swells. He finally topped the bluff to see below in the valley, the quaint little settlement of Dunkirk, and to the side of a crosswork pattern of gravel roads, bearing the fronts of shops, then a church and ballfield, then houses and yards, --was a lane that parlayed right off into a barnyard and parked round back at a pond. Ali stood still and summoned the gathering night up close to his ears. Amidst the settlings of dusk, there was a faint fiddle sound trickling up the hill and briskly cutting through the evening air like a cross cut saw on a jack pine, emitting a rhythmic canter that ebbed and flowed and dosey-doed..

Ali didn't know it but he was descending into Saturday night at a Dunkirk social. He strode down to the heart of the activity. Soon he perceived waving ribbons of chatter in different notes and tones –intertwining; some high and cheerful, some low and deliberating.. and many medium ones-- all engaged in a friendly little hum. The barn was beautiful.. big and old with barnswallows darting in and out of her friendly wide open hayloft. The wood was warbly and worn with shingles on the side that displayed rusty browns, reds and shadows of grey, tinged at every slant with gleamings under a big ol cornbread moon that had just passed full and was perched as if to serve as a hung lantern.   Two big wooden doors were propped and standing open, and the bustle inside was softly rolling and overflowing out into the evening air. How different Ali suddenly felt. A strange excitement overtook him, leaving thoughts of spirit for a moment. Then he quickly gathered it back to him, and smiling a big broad smile, stepped inside.

The barn was full of townspeople, some dancing..some sitting on bales of hay and benches. They clapped along to a feisty little 'shady grove' song fluttering down off a stone-boat stage at one end of the barn. It was lit by an open moon-beamed entrance from the hayloft above, and coal oil lamps were draped from the rafters. The boys on the stage wore a kindred spirit of concentration on their faces with heads tilted towards each other, embracing an invisible circle of enchantment. Their instruments gaily wailed and fully engaged the audience too, creating a current of life that continually and contentedly completed itself in the transference of joy-to-music, music-to-joy. Ali leaned against the wall at the back. He began finally to mingle with some clusters of folks, and felt welcome.

People began to be drawn to him. His eyes met every face with a genuine love, born from deep inside, and these folks were starting to gather where this new thrust of enthusiasm was being stirred up. A boy named Dalton introduced himself. He told Ali that it was a treat for them to have somebody all the way from Enoch come to one of their dances. Ali felt like he was suspended in the air. He kept feeding on the energy and could hardly contain the impulse he had to gather everybody up into his arms. Oh, Great One.. he whispered lightly.. what a variety you have made. How. wonderful! Dalton's dancing partner was a pretty girl named Angela. They circled the room in a two step, and returned again, breezing by their new found friend. Ali smiled. Dalton winked.

Ali felt emotions coming to the surface, out of their nest of serenity within. He began to let them feel little bursts of experience..after all, he didn't happen on a magic night like this very often. He thought this is what it must feel like to be drunk, and knew he would have to pay when the feisty little wave of adventure sunk to a trough later on and he would have to gather his essence back into its privacy like so much milk that had escaped through holes in a bucket. "Stay with me Sir".. he whispered to his Divine One.. "as much as you can. I know", he continued.. "that everybody is a window through which you are looking". And he continued to meet people, and listen to the sweet melodies.

"Lips as red as a bloomin' rose   Eyes of the deepest brown
You are the darlin' of my heart..   Stay till the sun goes down".

The moon above smiled through the hayloft and the whole dance hall seemed to be floating in a warm hum.

The fiddles lively flight began to fade into a delicate floating whisper as it mingled into the night with a soft refrain

"and the frost shows
    on the windows,   and the wood stove smokes and blows..

  and as the fire glows
we can warm our souls   chasing rainbows in- to gold..

  and we talked of
trails we walked off   far above the tim- ber line,

  and from that night on
I knew I'd write songs   of Carolina in the pines.."

The gay mood finally began to dwindle to a lull, and folks began to filter out of the dance hall. Ali had been talking with Dalton and a few younger folks at a picnic table. The conversation had come around to church the next morning, and

Dalton and Angela, Ali found, were very much devoted to the Lord too. They however, were much more verbal on the subject than Ali's people of Enoch were. Grandfather talked with him, but not so much in opinions as just ideas that opened up to the skies, and Ali would very often finish the thought by reading Grandfather's eyes. He was missing Grandfather, and wished these people could know of that kind of communication. It fondly came into his mind how, when he first wanted to strike out into nature on his own, he sought to find a look of consent. Grandfather had seemed secretly pleased. Ali was encouraged, and with eagerness looked up at his Grandparent asking "to become one with spirit, where shall I go?".. "Into the seam - that falls between.. the twilight and the rim".. Grandfather was gazing at the horizon, his eyes a pool of eternity. .

Well, Ali knew that he was closing in on that rim. This was part of it too. He was being careful to listen intently and project a loving intention into this event, for it was sacred. Dalton seemed to like him, and confided his most cherished thoughts on the teachings of Jesus. There was not so much room for Ali to interject revelations of his own, so he happily listened to this catechism lesson, and realized that it was indeed founded on truth. It seemed to him that there were many sides up a mountain , so long as God was there at the top.

Finally Dalton's father came to gather the family home. " Ali", he said.. "please stay the night with us. You can attend Sunday service and I will feel better letting you get a start back to your people in the light of the noonday sun". That night Ali slept in a little caravan-type travel- trailer in the back yard of Dalton's family home. It was very agreeable to him, and the pillow was soft. It was thrilling to be under new canopies and breathing the air of a different valley. He happily laid back, stretching his thoughts to see his little caravan 'dwelling' journeying among many others with beautiful colors of decoration-- far across distant shores and into the magical musical realm of Gypsies. He could hear the tinkling of haunting melodies he had known forever.. and he, the eternal wondering vagabond free there, in the days of old. "Oh beautiful Sir" he sighed.. "Thank you". He pulled the charming scene close in to him and yielding, it begin to swirl upward, thick like syrup at first and rich with inspiration. It finally found its upward flow and diluted into a stream out the top of his head as a gentle cool little wind. He drifted off as easily as a little papoose.

The cooing of doves woke him to the gleamings of a new day. There was a big breakfast of flapjacks and bacon, and Ali washed up in a real bathroom, and made his way back to the trailer, putting on a clean shirt from his traverse pack. He sat to meditate. A funny feeling began to invade him there.. the thought of being too worldly.. the thought of the aimless play of other kids his age back in his home prairie and how he used to also immerse himself in such things.

He quickly caught these thoughts. "It is just that I let the milk out of my bucket some".. he assured himself. And so, he took those feelings and corralled them in with the good ones; brothers to all.. and let them be thrown together into his upward meditation offering of the morning. Nothing but various energies, he mused.. thoughts that were dedicated in the past to different desires, curiosities and obligations. Or, silly little jealousies and competitions. I will let them go now, he determined. Then he mixed them all together like so much bannack batter; the tart salty baking soda mix with the floury sugar mix. Upward then to divine Mother to put in her oven. "The way to get rid of false identifications is to relax away from them", he affirmed, as he mentally released the aroma of the mixture and offered it joyfully up to her. The scent was sweet.. the good had overlapped the bad.. the sour had been blended in and transformed.

Ahh, he was looming there at the spiritual eye, comfortable in his little treetop perch. Suddenly there it was.. the bell. A beautiful rich deep gong very close by. A real church!

Presently he found himself seated in a fine little cathedral. The walls were high, and there were pillars, with a chiming organ and angelic choir voices. Ali's spirit was stirred as he withdrew into himself and opened up from his heart to his head, letting in the aroma that was generated here. It felt like the fresh breath of Jesus himself descending down into him. The statues that embroidered the walls and corners were so beautiful. They depicted Angels, Saints, and the Virgin Mother and child. The cross of Jesus adorned the alter. Ali felt free to let himself go inwardly and the intensity of a deep calmness embraced him affectionately, until his face beamed and his eyes sparkled. Later on he met with a circle of friends at the lane out front and bid a fond farewell, bouncing off happily down the road, across a ditch and into a pasture that stretched back up the hill.

By late afternoon, he stopped along the brook to commune with the Great One. The outward excitement of the past days he calmly grasped with his heart and directed up into submission. This practice was rather like when the kids used to swim at the canal back home. He would jump in off the access bridge above, and the water flowed swiftly over a concrete embankment below. It was challenging. You would hit the water, sinking way down. Then you'd get immediately sucked into a whirlpool formed by that wall and one about 15 feet directly out front; about 2 feet below the rushing water line. Within those 15 feet you had to scramble to find your direction within that turbulence, face frontward, take full control of your body within the force of that flow, and throw your feet out front so they could make first contact with the next concrete wall; stopping yourself from flying away down the stream. If you didn't catch the bar, you were lost. Your body could be thrown against and over it, possibly gashing your head open. But planting your feet first on it, you were able to stabilize and stand on the bar, carefully walking to the bank so you could 'yee-haw', and prepare to climb up onto the bridge and jump again.

Maybe the kids instinctively knew it was a good developing practice to use these tests as play sometimes. Ali thought about great Masters like Jesus finding themselves in intense circumstances and coping appropriately right there on the spot like that. What must it have been like when he was hanging up there on that cross.. For anyone who had attained a somewhat higher state of awareness, your mental citizens would rally to perform out of the arsenal of your finely tuned and perfected practices. The forces of love someone like he would have developed, would have to be impenetrable, and be summoned to the fore to shore up the advance. The energies that supported fear, despair, impatience, confusion, anger, or agony.. would be anhialated, and then ultimately transformed in that sudden battle, to their opposites. Ali supposed that in all possibility, someone highly evolved like Jesus, having bared down on impending doom and attacking it with love, may have indeed, actually felt a great surge of love and immense power from those latent hurtful qualities being quickly overcome in battle like that. He may have been swooning in the joy of all the power that had been unleashed for good. What an amazing thought..

Soon Ali's meditation began to succumb to the beauty of his surroundings filtering in. He was softened by the sun of his love, and the wind of his affection. He stayed there for a long time glowing in an exquisite feeling of belonging to it all. When his body alerted him that maybe it was time to move on, his soul was beginning to have a voice too, and chimed in softly.." no, there is nowhere I'd rather be than here. Why not take a moment to listen to nature's word of ecstasy.. listen closely in the right ear. Hear the faint cool breeze venturing in a little more surely to the forefront -and let it have the freedom to grow into a rushing vibration that happily explores into new little channels. The many chambers inside are relaxing into such joy; pleasantly awakening and opening up, until the flow is present everywhere --encompassing your whole body. Relax and let it continue, and you start to **become** it --seeing too, that what is inside you is the same as the succulent essence that you love in nature outside of you..and it will smile and show you further .."yes you have understood.. it is I.. the one that is present everywhere.. you have found me out"!. Finally you feel like your skin melts away.. there are no nerves, no tissues.. and you yourself simply becomes everything around you. The light too, that forms between your temples, if you gently encourage it, lets you in.. becoming more and more finely condensed until you see a perfect little white star directly before you, and with increasing sincere thrusts of devotion, can penetrate into it, finally being freed into a newly emerging vibrating ocean of light that pulsates and shimmers in effervescently pure rainbow hues. It is thrilling beyond description! "Oh..the great discoveries of Lewis and Clark didn't **begin** to touch on this kind of beauty"! Ali thought.. Yes, there was much to keep one occupied here.. how divinely beautiful. And he stayed much longer.

That evening, he lay back on his pelt and looked up into the night. How interesting it had been to be so close to people his own age who had such a different upbringing. He thought about Dalton, who was so thoughtful, and sincere about things. Yes, he thought, it could be Dalton laying here looking up at the sky as easily as I. Of course, he wouldn't be on a bear pelt..perhaps a saddle to rest his head upon.

He would be like me though, after finding glimmers of real peace, preferring the wide dark canopy of the prairie sky to a bunkhouse or teepee any day. How beautiful he would see the stars, just the way I do. They would remind him maybe as they do me, of that wonderful song that says **"When you wish upon a star.. makes no difference who you are.. Anything your heart desires will come to you"**. Makes no.. difference who you are. "Yes", thought Ali.. "when you gaze at the point between the eyebrows, there is a lighter feeling in the body. The star **will** form there whether your eyes are open or closed. It has five points with its little arms, legs and head. And as long as you gently nudge the energy to carry along in the upward direction when it starts to jiggle outward in excitement, or downward in sadness or confusion, then it will find its way back to this sweet spot every time, where one can see that star. And indeed, it is just like the expected result of wishing on a star to feel relief and see answers -simple and true, where there used to be only puzzling questions. How wonderful. ." He realized suddenly too, that "anything your heart desires will come to you" was a truth, as was "**your dream comes true**", for your magnetism develops within the subtler laws of attraction by your expressing love, and you ***attract*** lovely things to your life. And too, wishing, focusing, yearning.. penetrating –that finally frees you to emerge out of God's dream into a reality a thousand thousand times more real, vibrant and true..thus in that way, dreams really do become ***true***!

Ali sighed a deep contented sigh. His thoughts began to expand-- not only to Dalton, but to Angela, who was so pretty. Dalton did seem to care for her so much. And, as they danced together at the barn-dance, her step was graceful and carefully perfect within his. She followed with a dedicated loyalty to his confident lead. Well, that was all fine, but he wondered.. if Dalton became, so urgent like I am, in my search for the great Spirit, would Angela slow him down? After all, girls had to ***feel*** everything instead of logically pioneering new territory and discovering new clues along the path to get you farther. Girls will get too close to you, and then when you forget to pay attention to them, their feelings will be hurt and there's a halt in the whole business. He imagined if Dalton was as driven as he to get somewhere in his life, well, he compared the idea to a fast horse; focused on his goal and racing the wind to get there in record time. What then of Angela.. she would be riding the horse, keeping in balance with his gallop. What then, when he took a sharp turn unexpectedly? She may not be clever enough to know it was coming; distracted by the time it takes to always be consulting her ***feelings***. She would end up falling right off the horse. It would slow him down, or maybe he would even keep going, and .. leave her behind..

How can one progress in that way?? His thoughts then turned to his beloved friend back home; Mooksie. Oh how he missed her. She seemed to have just the right words or a tender look when he needed them most. She was devoted to him, and when he hurt her feelings he felt badly afterwards for a long time..even if he tried to glaze over the incident and reason it out as being just an ordinary little mistake. It hurt him to see her disheartened. He thought again, "where does a girl fit in to the quest to become part of the Great Spirit? How did Grandfather and Grandmother smooth out their reasoning and feeling differences, so that they fit together and complimented each other so well"? Or his own parents too,who set such a fine example..

He saw himself crafting his totem pole of devotion perfectly. It was a labor of love .. his offering would reach God..it would please him. Well, where would Mooksie fit in to that? She would not be able to build it the way he envisions it, and her preoccupation with feelings would leave her behind at the bottom again and again. The whole thing would tumble down ..

But, men and women are supposed to be together..why?

He wished he could be like an eagle and simply fly to God. How easy it would have been when he was an eagle. But, alas, the eagle didn't know there was a God. What good was being able to fly so high then? ..If only a person's soul could take to flight..how glorious the path to the Great Spirit would be. Then suddenly he thought of the *female* eagle. The mother. She would not let the hatchling leave the nest before it was ready.

No flying to God or anywhere for that matter, until the young ones had instinctually learned to steer the course. They had many experiences to pass through first, to sure them up for the leap into the skies of promise. Somehow the mother knew how to lead the way. Her feelings were intense and translated into unconditional love and loyalty. She would be the pole star to cling to that would some day land you in the vicinity of God. This is the power that was hidden dormant in Angela, and in Mooksie.. this potential of guidance. And having such an ability took a great deal of being in touch with your **feelings**. Perhaps the male **needed** the female nature with him to transform his reason into something more useful. And maybe that's why you take another with you to merge with the great Spirit. Sure, you can just try to get there yourself so you can do it quickly and efficiently, but.. wouldn't it be kind of like arriving in the heavens, to find that only a hand or foot break through.. Suddenly Ali saw the great fault in the thinking of the civilized world. It was right there in front of him. The Great Spirit

is all of us. When you give energy in the form of good will to another, you realize then; seeing this channel opening, that not only the source of what you ***give*** comes through here, but the life force you ***receive*** also – what you live on and depend on, comes through here as well. It is much bigger than just you. If you don't learn to share and live in others, you begin to feel bound by this little body, when there's something in the nature of the soul that wants to be in ***all*** bodies. The female nature is an integral part of learning to accomplish this. Perhaps the horse needs to concentrate on providing a nice ride, after all. Perhaps the faces on the totem pole should reflect the many who also want to share in the offering. We need each other. If I didn't someday take someone like Mooksie for a mate, he thought, I would have no one to care for.. no incentive or outward reason to forge a path; to experiment with making things better. There would be no nest to invite little baby souls to come and live with us. I wouldn't have the heart quality developed deeply enough for the journey to God..it would be closed off and constricted.. un-***tried***. With her love, and the pride I feel in doing for my family, I forge a glorious path indeed to the great Spirit, for all of us.. and in the satisfaction of taking care of these loved ones, I expand my sympathies to see that others in the village can indeed be loved ones too. In doing for others, I grow. I can help almost anyone finally, to get to the big Spirit in one way or another. By the magnetism I develop, they too will be drawn.. If it weren't so much more blissful to give than receive, I would never have the initiative to put one foot in front of the other on this path. Yes, the soft beautiful eyes of Mooksie stay in my dreams and carry me through rough waters. And my love for Grandfather won't let me fail. All the world needs help. Oh if my little family could strengthen and grow enough to be a great ship that could carry a multitude of discouraged wounded souls over the rough waters to the tranquil center of all that is."

Ali thought of the Saints throughout history he had spent long hours reading about in the library at the reservation. He imagined all those beautiful faces with eyes glowing upwardly in devotion. Many came from ancient times, and lands oceans away.. there was Krishna with his flute, the grand Buddha who would not give up until he swept the whole society of his day up into his wake, toward the golden shores of enlightenment. He remembered stories of great Shaman of his own people, that had come before Grandfather. He remembered his Grandfathers words saying that one moon gives more light than all the stars, and he saw Jesus again in his minds eye, then smiled to think how the wise men must have marveled upon seeing such a wonderous thing appear to their consciousness --as the star of an Avatar newly descending upon this earth in such a desperate time of need. What love had all these, for God. But again it entered Ali's thoughts..for the multitudes who are all destined to someday attain greatness, it will be **Mother** who shows them their first true and lasting love in the world. After all, even the Saints were at one time just people like Ali who hadn't started on the path home yet. What good would any of them have done, had they only tried to get themselves to the shores of peace, leaving everyone else behind? Anyone who ever did anything worth while came by way of a mother, Yes, the girl who becomes the mother.. she gives freely this first suckling love. And, in learning how to expand on that love, one sees what great worth there is in feelings to develop things along. Then he thought much more deeply, about God as a Divine Mother, giving birth in a profound gesture of generosity and joy; to a manifestation tumbling out as myriads of vast universes, existing of center everywhere, circumference nowhere! Each entity is in itself a unique expression of infinite creation. Ali marveled as he remembered hearing uttered once, a deep yet purely simple truth. For indeed, he thought, **the hand that rocks the cradle rules the world.**

PART II

Finding Happiness

Hours happily stretched into days spent with God in the all-embracing silence of divine grace, and Ali began to feel like a bird that had been looming near the open door of a cage. Not bothered any longer by the cold, or heat, or nagging thoughts.. the one goal presented itself ever more alluringly to him.. freedom. Why not.. just fly out. He felt like he lost time here and there, in the hours spent out of the silence and on the trail, but intuitively he knew he had been going for little test runs. And when he was back into the flow of meditation, his experience was ever richer and mounting in familiarity and purpose. He was feeling more and more at home here as the **watcher** of everything perceivable. He didn't exist but his experience did. And, when he felt the most released into the skies of freedom within, .. he really couldn't contemplate anything more than that. But he didn't need to because it felt so good. Intense.. existence was simply an intensely exquisite deep yearning at those times.

Finally one day, he decided to go home to see his teacher. There was much to do in the village. He had been able to overcome distractions and moods here. Now his religion could be tested in the cold light of day; everyday living with his people. Maybe he could help teach others someday as Grandfather was teaching and guiding him. After all, the world needed help. He knew very few people were searching for the great Spirit. But that they needed help was evident. There was great stress living in the world today, especially those sensitive enough to know there is something within their grasp that they are not yet subtly developed enough to begin the search for. Jesus said "What I have done, ye can do also". There is no other reason for living than to achieve it. Many are keenly aware of the suffering of their separation from the vast oneness of spirit. But, they have no idea what to do about it. Ali knew that even from breaking through a little himself, his countenance among the others would be a strong influence and support for them. It would begin to magnetize them; like a paper clip set next to a bar magnet. Finally the little clip becomes a magnet itself. Oh, how he missed Grandfather. He set off for home.

When he started to feel the vicinity of his valley was near, the appearance of each familiar surrounding was dearly welcome to his heart. Every tree and waving cluster of grasses were long missed friends saying "hello, welcome home"..The birds sang swells of crescendoing gladness for his being once again among them. The boy was coming home from the forest. He stepped into a clearing and suddenly was confronted head on, by a wolf. Ali stopped and calmly looked at him. Oh, the poor fellow.. his ribs were showing through and his fur was scarred and disheveled. The wolfs eyes became instantly frightened, and he skulked off hurriedly. Instead of being relieved to have avoided him, Ali was filled with love for him. He almost wished he had a rabbit to offer.. he would gladly take on the responsibility now for slaying one, if it could have helped the poor wolf. How different the expectations of meeting a wolf had become..he marveled. Finally he was home.

....

Home, here and now. And a thought that you, dear faithful reader of this story; you who have remained with him all the way through to the end thus far.. For this glorious reunion, perhaps we could tune in if we are very still and listen carefully, to Ali's own thoughts and words as he experiences the wondrous last leg of his journey.

"Then over the hill I saw the tall thin form of the one whose every movement is etched in my mind..the one whose voice is thrilling to me. "Grandfather"! I cried and ran to to the arms of my beloved teacher. I saw a tear in my Grandfather's eye as he quickly gathered me up in his arms.."Oh, my own " I heard in his whisper. Then he stiffened and set me to arms length looking deeply at me. "You have grown".

I had so much to tell him. But for now, I centered myself and smiled. We walked to the corrals together, and threw a couple of bails over the fence to some yearlings. "Grandfather", I said later as we sat to drink some sassafras root beer Grandmother brought to the bench under the willow grove. . "I spent some time at Dunkirk settlement. There was a church there, and I went in. Afterwards I went into the deep silence. It had so affected me being there, that I sought once again to see Jesus, the great Master of that land. Many times I have felt the yearning to find him after hearing his Bible stories. There was a boy, and girl about my age, and they spoke of him so affectionately..well, I wanted to know him like they did.

The thing is Grandfather, they told me he is the only one. What does that mean to be the only **one**? Well, God is the "one" creation itself **comes from** -he answered. Not the person Jesus, he went on, but what he has acquired in realization, is the consciousness of God itself. He was able to merge into spirit. He became a cause, and not just an effect. His being is an initiation of purpose in this world; divine grace in action, not merely **re**-actions to circumstances. Grandfather looked skyward and said "You know how the sky looks in the dark with all that glows and sings in the night..worlds upon worlds as far as the eye can see, and farther still? "Yes Sir" I said. He looked at me with raised eyebrows. "Do you suppose we are the only ones in this whole vast existence.. with all that life teeming out there.. everywhere"? He grinned. "This great Master Jesus Christ broke through the little self into the great Spirit beyond. He found out how to tap into and harness great stores of power that he could use to help people. But, you see Ali, he came at a time when people couldn't imagine in ways we can today. There are much larger universes in orbit out there that solar systems are only part of. When our larger universe is close in its orbit to the dual suns at its core, its magnetic properties are very strong, and its subtle energies are very high. People know no time nor space then. We are closer in this orbit now, than when Jesus was in the world. Most people then couldn't understand energy the way we can now. Jesus draws power freely from the source and lives by the higher laws of the Great Spirit. Even science will, in time catch up to the understanding of these intrinsic but simple laws of attraction. When he was here, he taught many truths to those who travelled and lived with him. Just as I do with you. I too have broken somewhat through the little self and am touching the hem of the garment of the great Spirit." I thought of the grand ceremony of my dream and smiled. "This isn't my first rodeo, you know.". Grandpa smiled back. . Then he paused, looking at me. "Nor is it yours," he added. "You didn't happen to be my grandson by accident. We have been together many times before, because I show you things. So, my little grown one, I can teach you like the Master Jesus taught, and like other Masters have taught as well, through the ages. Much of the civilized world knows Jesus best, because in history he has been the most loved of the ones who have been here most recently. He came at a time of such deep yearning by people who were feeling separated and lost. His love was very.. **VERY** great".

Then Grandfather's voice softened. "I can teach you what he wants you to know. His love can come through me to you, for aren't we both part of the great Spirit after all? And too, Jesus may have come here to help many times in other bodies as well, for those dedicated to helping mankind will stop at nothing. Your little friends said he was the only one..well, they misunderstood just a little. He is "ONE"..period. For creation to exist, that one consciousness had to vibrate itself to propel out a force that could "be" a creation. When you see a ripple in water, it is the one point vibrating out to become many reflections of that one point. When you see a windmill moving in the wind, it looks like a disc. But to see it in the stillness, you see it is only one bar of wood..not many making a circle. It is only one. Creation is the vibration of one to assume the role of many, as in a dream or a play. We are a dream within the Great Spirit seeking to return so that we may create on our own. Instead of just being in a dream, we will, dear one..we MUST..become the dreamer too. Sound manifests outward from the sacred silence at the center. Movement emerges from perfect stillness at the center.. God is the Great Spirit at the center. That center is the only ONE thing that is real. To create is to introduce intent; activate potential..thoughts vibrate into activity – and that becomes matter in its farthest reaches - even to the point of inertia in the rocks. The projection of energy produces fluctuations as waves are upon an ocean.. ups and down, highs –lows, love-hate, joy -sorrow and so on. For every wave in this duality of creation, there is a trough. But if one can rise above it all and not be so involved in the dream of creation..one can maintain the panoramic view where there is just ocean, still and calm. We can withdraw, like you have learned in your quest for truth. You've begun to feel and experience much more deeply from that point of stillness you discovered within. You have found the great Spirit at the center of creation that has become that creation." Grandfather laughed. "You are starting to see behind the scenes. But, this is what Jesus meant when he said The Lord God is One; that one consciousness that created

Creation itself. Thus when you have merged into God, you can say "I AM ONE"."Yes", I said.. my heart tingling.."I AM ONE..I know what you mean now". It was all coming to me as if a beautiful memory from eons ago. "Yes, I am at the core of all that is..this is what I truly am".

"Are you ready for the ceremony tomorrow", Grandfather asked? " Even at your tender age, you have become wise. You have become a man". Ali looked down and said "Grandfather.., I.. didn't even hunt.." "I know" said Grandfather. Then he turned his glance upward so the sunlight caught him on the cheek, and brightened his eyes.."Like I said, you have become a man..You will be given a new name". "What will it be"?
"Well, Aliheli means happy. You will now have the added name of Tsi Da. Aliheli-Tsi Da! Your name has changed from Happy to "HappiNESS".
There is a big difference".
Grandfather's eyes twinkled.

THE END

PART III

Once in a great while,
when you've earned it
You find someone,
who can teach you

Learn of the incredible life of Swami Kriyananda;
J. Donald Walters,
at www.Ananda.org
Or you may look for youtube videos
under the author's name;
sharon lenore anderson

LAST LETTERS FROM SWAMI

This book; "Between the Twilight and the Rim" was written not long before Swami passed. It was largely inspired by a novel he had just written – the most wonderful story I have ever read. It turned out to be his swan song, in a way. It was called

Love Perfected, Life Divine: A Novel
Swami Kriyananda

Inspired by Marie Corelli's book, Kriyananda retells the dramatic story of a woman's discovery of her twin soul—which propels her to undertake an arduous and perilous climb to the loftiest heights of spiritual awakening.

When little Ali thought of his Grandfather, it was easy to convey that pure love, for it was my love for Swami.

The next year after his death I made a pilgrimage to the gravesite at his Ananda Hermitage in California, and sat there on the little grassy patch outside his patio, facing the magnificent Sierra Nevada canyon that cascaded across the skyline there, and landed at the Yuba river, curling through the forest at the bottom. Hawks were circling above, and there was a deep serenity pervading us there, Swami and I. His picture sat in front of a simple statue of Master, and he was enjoying the last year in his yard before the body would be transported to the temple being built in his honor not many yards away, down what had been part of his lower driveway.

There I read this book out loud.. well half of it. I felt such peace and his companionship there, and wanted to share with you, dear reader.. the tranquility I found. I have made this reading available and the link is mentioned on the last page. The reading was afterward completed right on that sacred river that flowed below the canyon, and I inserted Swami's own instrumental music as a backdrop. His magnetism is palpable in this reading and I urge you, if you enjoy this offering, to use the companion mp3 reading. It will I think, inspire you.

Swami's influence on me is what propelled me to write any and all of my creative spiritual content --whether it be in the form of song, video, commentary or book.

Parts of his last correspondence with me I am sharing with you as a conclusion to this little book. A conclusion yes, and the remnants of my contact with him in his body.
But the beginning only, to a relationship that sweepingly grows brighter, broader and more beautiful with each passing day.

Dear Swami,

When you were feeling so rough these past few days, I tried so hard to be there for you. It occurred to me that I had been writing a little novel a couple or more weeks ago.. around the time you were perhaps writing yours.. anyway, before I was so profoundly affected by yours, I had amazingly been somewhat attuned! Well I took out the draft this morning and redding it — was quite pleased — thinking yes — perhaps this could lift your spirits some if you care to take a look. So I'm going to finish it up this weekend. What inspired it (besides you, of course) was the thought of writing a story line that could make use of some of Ollie's little indian pictures.

    I love you sir, and think of you all the time. Thanks for giving us the Dream ship to find you on, and all the tests that make us better.

                         Yours in Master,
                              Sharon

Dear Sharon:

Your beautiful and sweet letter gave me a chuckle this morning. You are so dear. I'm glad you enjoyed my novel and that it inspired you to finish writing yours. I only read a few pages of it because Miriam only printed a few to show me. However, I look forward to reading the rest of it. Ollie's pictures are perfect. You make a good team: writer and illustrator.

love,
swami   NK/nm   Wed, Mar 20, 2013 09:30 AM
And, his last comment ever, to me:

Your sincere and sweet devotion to God and Guru is
the highest I would ever want or expect from one of my
very own,
as indeed, you are.

love,
swami

NK/nm   Sent: Tue, 16 Apr 2013 07:08:41

Swami Kriyananda
May 19, 1926 to April 21, 2013

Look for the Yogananda movie; "Awake".
Also the movies that have been written By Swami Kriyananda;
"The Answer", "The Wayshower", and "Finding Happiness"

Here is one of Swami's many books,
this one a fun adventure,
with many deep truths within its pages.

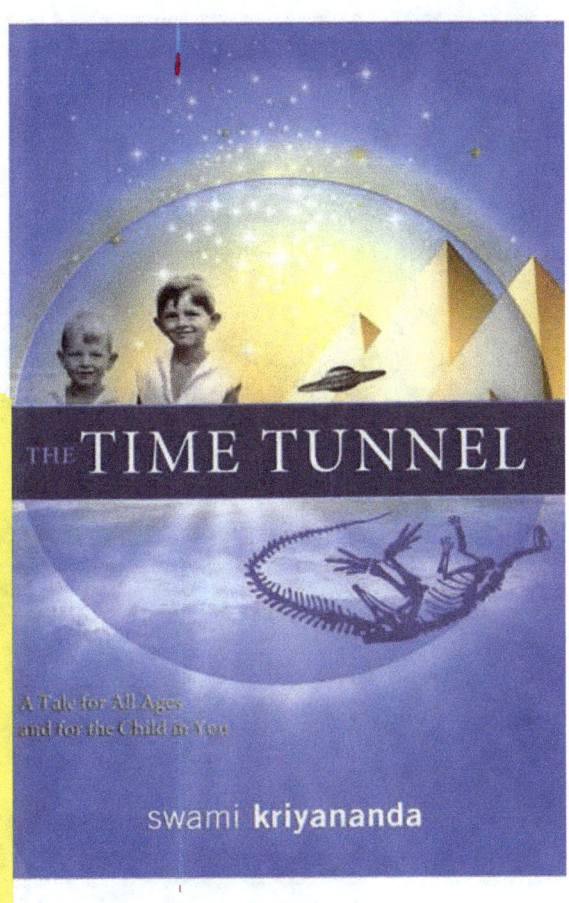

Swami Kriyananda is a world-renowned spiritual teacher and composer who has authored more than 140 books, including *Stories of Mukunda* episodes from the boyhood of Kriyananda's guru, the great world teacher, Paramhansa Yogananda) and *Education for Life* (a treatise on modern education that serves as the foundation for the popular Living Wisdom Schools). Along with the Dalai Lama and Jane Goodall, Kriyananda is a member of the prestigious Club of Budapest. His autobiography, *The New Path*, won the 2010 Eric Hoffer Award.

THE TIME TUNNEL

While exploring in Romania, brothers Donny and Bobby discover a ruined laboratory with a mysterious tunnel. Entering into it, their bodies shrink. They emerge into a beautiful countryside and meet Hansel, whose father invented the "time tunnel." After Hansel shows the boys how to encase themselves in time-light spheres, the trio journeys through time—visiting the Middle Ages, ancient Greece and Egypt, and forward into a surprising future. Along the way the boys gain valuable lessons about history, human behavior, and themselves.

"A charming tale that whisks the reader through time and space, imparting gems of wisdom along the way."

—Michael Sussman, author of the visionary novel, *Crashing Eden*

"Captivating and magical."

—Shankari Boldt, retired middle-school teacher

"*The Time Tunnel* will take you to Atlantis, ancient Egypt, and the future, as you never imagined them."

—Peggy Payne, author of *Sister India* and *Cobalt Blue*

"I think we've found another classic."

—Devi Novak, teacher, author of *Faith Is My Armor*

Swami Kriyananda is a direct disciple of the great world teacher, Paramhansa Yogananda. He has written more than 140 books, including *Stories of Mukunda* and *Education for Life*.

If these stories have intrigued the adventurer in you,
then here is a must for further reading.
It is exciting and mind expanding; unveiling concepts
that can now be understood in our scientific realms.
These studies are well documented and verified by some of the
greatest thinkers we have known of.

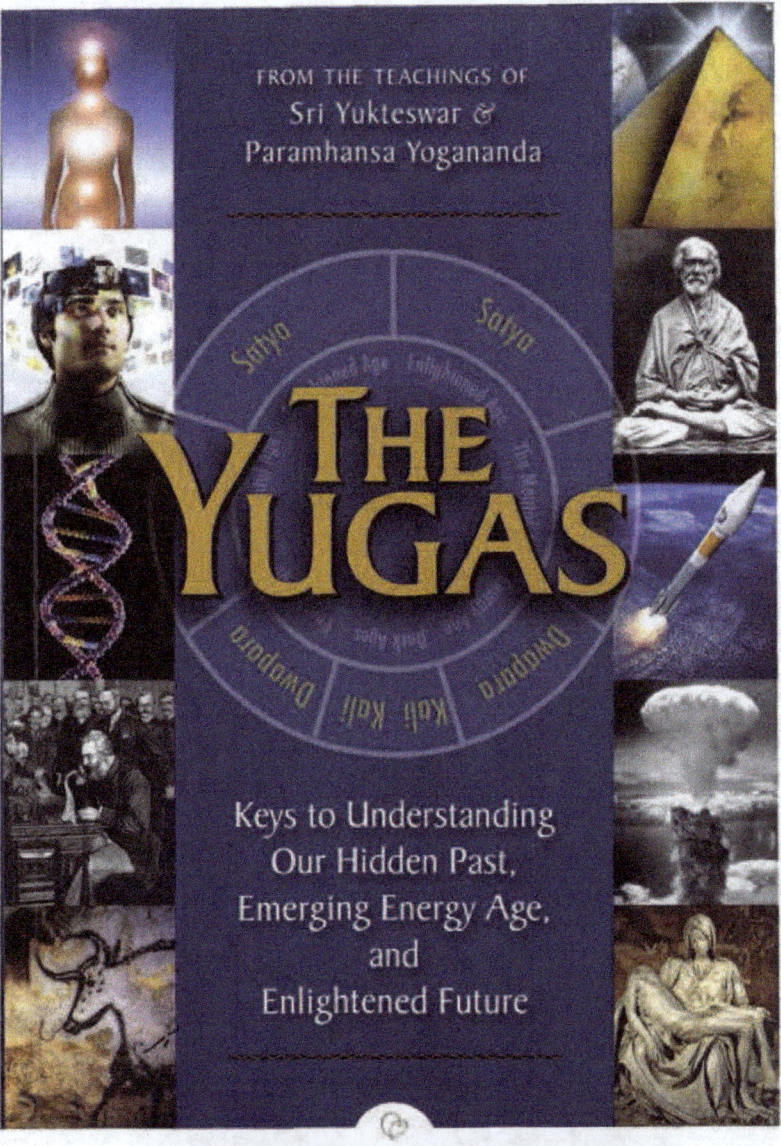

Read more about *The Yugas* and author events related to this book at:
www.theyugas.com

Millions are wondering what the future holds for mankind, and if we are soon due for a world-changing global shift. Paramhansa Yogananda (author of the classic *Autobiography of a Yogi*) and his teacher, Sri Yukteswar, offered key insights into this subject. They presented a fascinating explanation of the rising and falling eras that our planet cycles through every 24,000 years. According to their teachings, we have recently passed through the low ebb in that cycle and are moving to a higher age — an Energy Age that will revolutionize the world. Over one hundred years ago Yukteswar predicted that we would live in a time of extraordinary change, and that much that we believe to be fixed and true — our entire way of looking at the world — would be transformed and uplifted. In *The Yugas*, authors Selbie and Steinmetz present substantial and intriguing evidence from the findings of historians and scientists that demonstrate the truth of Yukteswar's and Yogananda's revelations.

"An amazing, mind-expanding investigation of the hidden cycles underlying the rise and fall of civilizations. I found *The Yugas* not only intellectually convincing but also spiritually and emotionally uplifting and deeply healing as well. Despite the dark signs of the times we live in, there is hope here for all of us." — **Graham Hancock**, author of *Fingerprints of the Gods*

"The conventional mainstream view of an overall linear progression in human history is no longer tenable; it is now clear that the ancients of 10,000 to 15,000 years ago were not 'primitives' and we have much to learn from them. This is a profound book... It provides new revelations on the unfolding of human potential over the course of millenia." — **Robert M. Schoch, PhD**, author of *Pyramid Quest: Secrets of the Great Pyramid and the Dawn of Civilization.*

"Selbie and Steinmetz have, in my opinion, produced a work of genius. If you aren't satisfied with what you've read, or been taught, about the linear development of civilization, you will find in this book an alternate picture of our Earth's history that will, I think, thrill you."
— **Swami Kriyananda**, author of *The New Path*

"Move over Copernicus, another revolution is underway! *The Yugas* will not only change the way we look at history, it will change the way we see ourselves and the world around us. This is a wisdom whose time has come. The startling revelations and sweeping vision of Selbie and Steinmetz deliver a story so timeless it will challenge and inspire generations to come!"
— **Walter Cruttenden**, author of *Lost Star of Myth and Time*

"Casts an important new light on the history and evolution of the human race and the mysteries of the great cycles of time that we must all honor. All those who want to understand our species and the hidden cosmic influences that govern our lives will benefit from its detailed examination. Those who study the book carefully will come away with a transformed vision of our world and its spiritual potentials." — **Dr. David Frawley (Pandit Vamadeva Shastri)**, author of *Astrology of the Seers* and *Yoga and Ayurveda*

Why I recommend "The Yugas"

Certainly I am no scholar. Not even close. I can only claim to having been captivated by a new way of thinking, endorsed by my perceptions in meditation. In this spirit then, I will share my findings with you as a friend and fellow seeker.

Two students of Swami Kriyananda/ Yogananda have compiled a compelling book called "The Yugas"; explaining an orbit Science is becoming better perched to understand in this; the (ascending) second of four "ages" experienced every 24,000 years. Many civilizations have referred to these ages, for example as Bronze, Copper, Silver and Golden, and have told of the higher ones existing in the past. That's because progress is not linear. We pass through higher ages and gradually fall into lower ones again and again. Our world is in a cyclical procession, becoming more magnetized and thus more subtly charged with energy from its influencing central creative thrust, as the galaxy gets closer to that center in its orbit.

At the closest point, humans existing here are more enlightened and communicate telepathically. Finally time and space are no longer experienced at all.

The ages then start to become dimmer again, and more "matter" conscious, as the galaxy descends in its orbit, away from the intensity of that central thrust. Thus our history holds higher ages as well as darker, lower ones. This world is not as it seems. Matter is at its root energy, energy – thoughts and ideas, thoughts and ideas—consciousness. That consciousness pervades all and is the creative thrust itself, of all that is.

We are in the second Yuga right now; Dwaparayuga. And that in itself is motivation to want to learn of the wonderful concepts all the great scriptural writings and Masters have alluded to. From great thinkers like Copernicus, to Einstein, and within so many others, were these intuitions budding. Today, much that seemed enveloped in secret shroud is now being unleashed and absorbed into a fresh awareness.

The remainder of this book presents a peek into "The Yugas"

Introduction

In 1905 Albert Einstein turned the world of physics upside down — for the first time the world saw the now famous equation, $E=mc^2$. Einstein fundamentally altered our understanding of the physical universe by proving that all matter was essentially condensed energy.

The nineteenth century view of the physical world was primarily mechanical; all matter was considered solid and fundamentally immutable. Although matter was considered to be made up of infinitesimally small objects, these were seen as solid objects nonetheless, and were believed to obey the same basic laws as did the sun and the planets. Time, too, was thought to be an unyielding constant throughout the universe, unaffected by changing conditions. In the nineteenth century the universe was seen as a very large machine, a clockwork of infinite size, functioning precisely and inexorably in its slow grandeur.

Today we hold a very different view of the physical world. All matter is understood to be energy in a condensed form. Not only do we consider matter mutable, we know that the tiniest atom is capable of being transmuted into vast amounts of energy. Both the incredibly destructive force of nuclear weapons, and the prodigious energy of nuclear power, testify to the profound implications of the deceptively simple equation $E=mc^2$.

Our view of the larger universe has also undergone a revolution. We now know that objects in space do not move in straight lines — because there *are* no straight lines. Space itself is curved and the universe is finite. No physical object can go faster than the speed of light. The speed of light is, in fact, the only constant in the universe — all else is measurable only in relation to that constant. Even time is understood to be relative to light.

The atom, previously conceived of as a constellation of tiny objects, like a miniature solar system with the nucleus taking the place of the sun (you probably made a model of one in sixth grade), has given way to a concept that cannot even be visualized. Physicists now conceive of the atom as a tiny area of space in which objects wink into and out of the quantum, subatomic world — a world where the very act of trying to observe the atom actually changes what is observed. Niels Bohr, the eminent early twentieth-century physicist and Nobel Prize winner, called the quantum world Potentia. Others have referred to it as quantum flux or quantum foam, an energetic maelstrom just below the threshold of measurable perception.

String theory, the latest "theory of everything," goes even further. String theory posits that there are no actual physical structures at all, that even the unimaginably small sub-atomic structures that physicists try to study, such as quarks, are, in reality, made up of even smaller vibrating strings and rings of energy.

Just a little more than a hundred years ago we understood our world to be made up of matter, interacted with by energy. Now we understand our world to be made up of energy, assuming the form of matter.

Acknowledgements

This book could not have been written were it not for Sri Yukteswar and Paramhansa Yogananda. Their twentieth century writings and teachings led the way in making the ancient teachings of India understandable to the Western mind. The significance of the yugas, in particular, had become lost in Indian tradition, but these two great souls presented the yugas anew, in simple clarity, giving them fresh relevance to our modern energy age.

This book also owes a great debt to the many talks and articles of Swami Kriyananda (J. Donald Walters) on the impact and qualities of the yugas. He has added rich dimension and depth of detail to our understanding of the yugas.

We would also like to acknowledge the legions of scientists and researchers willing to explore beyond orthodoxy—be they archeologists, professionals, and gifted amateurs alike, who are not satisfied with the standard linear theory of human development, or doctors and biologists, who are not satisfied with the standard material theory of human consciousness. Their dedicated work, and their thousands of books, articles, and lectures, present for all to see an astonishing number of unsolved mysteries of the ancient past, and fundamental gaps in our modern understanding of man.

Foreword
By Swami Kriyananda

I am sincerely pleased to be able to recommend this book, with enthusiastic applause. The subject has long interested me—indeed, from my youth. But I am deeply impressed by the depth of research and the astuteness with which the authors have approached their subject. I have written several books myself that included some of the points contained here, but this book goes far beyond my own minor contribution to the subject.

It was Swami Sri Yukteswar, in his book *The Holy Science*, who first propounded this revolutionary explanation for changes that have occurred in human consciousness over the centuries. I had already written a "source theme" in high school for my English class, when I was sixteen, which showed my fascination even then with ancient civilizations. Not to belabor what may seem a purely personal point of view, what interested me then, and what interests me as much today nearly seventy years later, is that I found the traditional explanation for ancient civilizations wholly unsatisfactory. It made (and makes) no sense to me for mankind to have spent many thousands of years as a "hunter and gatherer," and then suddenly to appear in a mere instant, so to speak, as the founder of great civilizations, complete with cities, industries, literature, education, and sophisticated cosmologies.

The name I chose for my source theme went something like this: "Ancient civilizations and their view of the universe." (I had wanted to study, further, what it was in those civilizations that had influenced people to develop those views, but here I was forced to admit failure; I could discover no such subjective influences.)

Mankind must, from the start, have had all the intelligence he needed to build cities and, with them, the appurtenances of a sophisticated civilization. Indeed, I'd read that the brain capacity of Cro-Magnon Man was larger than our own. And I wondered, on reading Egyptian history, how it happened that such a mighty civilization, after building the great pyramids, had descended to the level of mediocrity that has been evident in historic times. I simply wasn't convinced by the conclusions reached by the historians, developed from the data they had gathered. In fact, the more I read their conclusions, the more I inclined to agree with Napoleon's statement, "History is a lie agreed upon."

One thing that bothered me about the insights of so many historians, antiquarians, and other "specialists" was that they allowed facts to assume a separate reality of their own, seeming quite inadequate in their understanding of human nature. It was as if their approach to history had been only to gather those facts, but to make no attempt to place themselves actually in the shoes of the people they wrote about.

One wonderful thing about Sri Yukteswar's revelations (and to me they did in fact seem revelatory) was that he wrote at a time when a descending cycle of enlightenment—as described in this book—could be observed merging historically into an ascending cycle, and bringing radical change in human awareness with the birth of our present era, or *yuga*, of energy. Many facts of history over the last three thousand years are more or less known. Sri Yukteswar's explanation of those facts was, for me, deeply satisfying. This book presents his thesis with crystal clarity.

Selbie and Steinmetz have, in my opinion, produced a work of genius. They have gone, I think, as deeply into this subject as present-day knowledge permits. I am convinced that, living as we do in a cosmic environment, and one infinitely greater, therefore, than our environment on this little Earth, we are influenced also by that larger environment. We cannot but be affected: not only in our weather, but even in our consciousness. I am persuaded that many changes in human awareness take place not only because of the accretion of knowledge, but also in response to waves of conscious energy flowing into our planet from outside. For I believe that cosmic energy affects even human intelligence and awareness.

I am so enthusiastic on these points, indeed, that my very interest might induce me to repeat some of the points so excellently covered in this book! Let me therefore bow off the stage at this point, with only this comment: If you aren't satisfied with what you've read, or been taught, about the linear development of civilization, you will find in this book an alternate picture of our Earth's history that will, I think, thrill you.

Here are some other books
Sharon has written,
inspired also by the teachings of
Swami Kriyananda/Yogananda

you can find video, music,
and commentaries from Sharon
on the web at
www.youtube.com/SharonLenoreAnderson
www.SharonAndersonMusic.com
or www.SharonLenoreAnderson.com.

a free *audio reading* download for this book by the author can be found at the website above, under a tab called "AudioBooks"
the youtube site also has a slideshow and reading

email: sharon_L_anderson@comcast.net

www.ingramcontent.com/pod-product-compliance
Lightning Source LLC
Chambersburg PA
CBHW052136010526
44113CB00036B/2285